# SHARKS!
# SHARKS!
# SHARKS!

# SHARKS! SHARKS! SHARKS!

Happy Fox
BOOKS

written by
**SUSAN MARTINEAU**

illustrated by
**VICKY BARKER**

For Alice and Will, my very own fact finders! - S.M

For Harrison, who really loves sharks! - V.B

Paperback ISBN 978-1-64124-363-6
Hardcover ISBN 978-1-64124-364-3

Library of Congress Control Number: 2023947258

To learn more about the other great books from Fox Chapel Publishing, or to find a retailer near you, call toll-free
800-457-9112 or visit us at www.FoxChapelPublishing.com.

We are always looking for talented authors. To submit an idea, please send a brief inquiry to
acquisitions@foxchapelpublishing.com.

Fox Chapel Publishing makes every effort to use environmentally friendly paper for printing.

Printed in China

# Contents

# What is a shark?

Sharks are fish, and they live in all the world's oceans. Their bodies are perfect for hunting and surviving in the warmest or coldest seas.

Shark skeletons are not made of bone, but of bendy, gristly stuff called **cartilage**. Our ears are made of this too!

A shark's liver is big and oily. This helps the shark float. Some sharks can survive for a year without eating. They just live off the oil stored in their liver.

**Cartilage** does not weigh as much as bone. It helps a shark float and swim a long way without using up too much energy.

Many sharks have a slim shape that helps them move quickly through the water.

The fastest known shark is the **shortfin mako shark**. It can also leap really high out of the water!

**Dorsal fin**

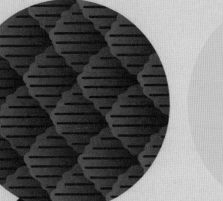

Sharks have hard, overlapping scales called **denticles**. These make shark's skin pointy and rough like sandpaper.

The **bramble shark** has such spiky **denticles** that they are like thorns!

Like humans, sharks need to breathe in a gas called **oxygen** to stay alive.

Most sharks have five slits on each side of their head. Under these slits are gills which help sharks breathe.

**Pectoral fin**

Water comes into a shark's mouth and out again through the slits. It passes over the gills which take in **oxygen** from the water.

# All sorts of sharks

When we think of sharks, we often imagine huge and scary creatures, but sharks come in all shapes and sizes. Some are really tiny, but others are the biggest fish on the planet!

The **whale shark** is the BIGGEST fish on Earth. It can grow as long as a bus.

The biggest whale shark seen so far measured 59 feet (18 m) long.

The **great white shark** can grow up to 20 feet (6 m) long. Its MASSIVE jaws can swallow a whole seal in one GULP!

The teeny **dwarf lanternshark** is so small that it can fit in the palm of a hand.

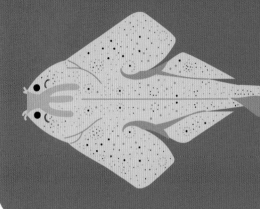

**Bullhead sharks** have very blunt heads and small spines on their **dorsal fins**.

**Angel sharks** have beautiful fins that look just like wings.

Some sharks have incredibly long tails. The **thresher shark** stuns the fish it likes to eat with its long, whippy tail.

There are hundreds of different kinds of sharks, but there may be even more that we have never seen—yet!

9

# Sharks have superpowers!

Sharks are the top hunters in the oceans. They can smell, hear, and see really well and have other amazing powers, too.

Many sharks have really big eyes. They can even see very well in the dark. Although they look different from ours, shark eyes have lenses, corneas, pupils, irises, and retinas, just like a human's!

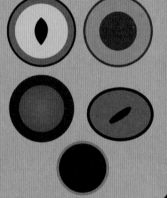

**Hammerhead sharks** have eyes on each side of their strangely shaped heads. They can see in all directions because their eyes point sideways. Very handy!

Sharks can smell blood in the water from a quarter of a mile away. That is very scary if you are an injured sea creature.

Electrical signals are given off by all living creatures as they move around. Sharks can sense them with special tiny pits on their noses.

These are sensors which detect the electrical signals so the shark knows exactly where its **prey** is moving.

The sensors are called **ampullae of Lorenzini**. What an amazing name for an incredible superpower!

Yikes! How did you know I was here?

Sharks that live near the bottom of the sea have **barbels**. These are like special whiskers that pick up the tiny vibrations made by the tasty creatures lurking under the seabed.

**Nurse sharks** have **barbels**.

11

# Chomp chomp!

Some sharks hunt, and others lie in wait to grab their **prey**. All sharks eat meat, and the shape of their teeth depends on what they like to eat best.

**Bullhead sharks**, like the **Port Jackson shark**, have back teeth shaped like pebbles. These can crush the shells of shellfish.

The **goblin shark** has very sharp, pointed teeth at the front of its long, scary-looking snout. It uses them to stab fish and squid.

**Basking sharks** have very small teeth because they don't really need them for chewing or chomping. They filter their food out of the water instead.

**Great white sharks** have about 300 triangle-shaped teeth with jagged edges for tearing chunks out of their **prey**.

2.4 inches (6 cm)

The **saw shark** has pointed teeth on both sides of its snout. These are perfect for digging food out of mud and sand.

Sharks have several rows of teeth in their jaws. When the front ones fall out, new ones in the row behind take their place.

A shark can get through THOUSANDS of teeth during its life.

The **snaggletooth shark** has the wonkiest teeth of all sharks! Their upper teeth are serrated (have jagged edges) and their bottom teeth are hooked. They use their teeth to tear apart prey.

You might even find a shark's tooth next time you are on a beach!

# Sharks don't really want to eat us!

Some sharks are more dangerous than others, but most sharks really do not want to eat us. They prefer to eat other creatures.

Shark attacks always make the news, but sharks do not kill many people each year.

There are just a few sharks that are known to attack humans ...

The **bull shark** hunts in warm, shallow water where humans also like to swim and play.

**Bull sharks** are very fierce hunters and can charge like a bull. They can also swim up rivers and will eat just about anything with their razor-sharp teeth.

The **tiger shark** can swim in very shallow water. It is able to come right up to the beach. It will also eat anything, including tin cans, car tires, and shoes.

The **great white shark** is the largest of all the sharks that sometimes attack people.

A surfer paddling on a board looks a bit like a tasty seal to a **great white shark** swimming underneath.

Sharks do not have a very good sense of taste. Sometimes they take a bite to see if they like what they are eating. Some shark attacks may be taste tests.

# Baby sharks

Mother sharks look for safe places, like reefs and coves, to have their babies. The babies are in danger of being eaten by many **predators** like dolphins, sea lions, or even other sharks.

Shark babies start life in different ways ...

**1.**

Some shark mothers lay eggs with baby sharks growing inside them.

The strong egg cases have long threads, which stick on to rocks or twine around seaweed to stop them from floating away.

The growing baby shark is called an **embryo**.

The **embryo** feeds on the yolk inside the egg case until it is ready to hatch.

The **Port Jackson shark** has egg cases shaped like a spiral. The mother shark wedges them under rocks to keep safe.

You can sometimes find shark egg cases on the beach. They are often called "mermaid's purses."

2.

Other shark mothers give birth to live baby sharks.

Shark babies are called pups!

**Blue sharks** can have over 100 pups at a time. The **great white shark** only has one or two.

Bye Mom!

**Great white sharks** are 5 feet (1.5 m) long when they are born. They have to look after themselves right away!

# Nursery time

Mangrove pools are the perfect nurseries for baby **lemon sharks**. Their mothers leave them there to grow up safely.

The mother **lemon sharks** swim into the mangrove pools when the water is high. They give birth to their pups, but they must leave before the water goes back out again.

The pools are not big enough for the mother sharks, but they are just the right size for the pups.

The little pups must fend for themselves, but this is a safe place for them to grow and learn to hunt for their food.

18

Mangroves are trees that form forests along the seashore or riverbank. They can grow in salty water.

Tangled roots

It is difficult for any bigger sharks to get in to harm them.

They learn how to hunt fish before it is time for them to leave for the open sea.

When it is time for them to have their own babies, **lemon shark** mothers return to the mangrove pools where they were born.

# Stripes, spots, and patterns

Some sharks are very hard to spot if you are a little fish swimming near them. Their color and shape help them **camouflage** themselves. This means they blend into their surroundings.

Many sharks have pale tummies and dark backs. It makes them very tricky to see from underneath, against the light coming down through the water.

**Pyjama sharks** have beautiful stripes running down their bodies.

I'm also called a **striped catshark** because of my whiskery **barbels**.

**Tasselled wobbegong**

**Wobbegongs** are **carpet sharks**. They have patterned bodies and flaps of skin around their heads and mouth. They look like a rug with bangs.

They blend in perfectly with the coral reefs where they live!

**Spotted wobbegong**

**Ornate wobbegong**

The **leopard shark** has a yellowish-brown body covered in dark-brown spots.

**Zebra shark** babies have stripes that gradually turn into spots as they grow.

SNAP!

**Angel sharks** have wide, flat bodies and broad fins that blend in with the seabed. They lie in wait for their **prey**.

The **dark shyshark** not only blends in on rocky seabeds, but it even curls into a ring to cover its eyes when it feels in danger.

# Coral reef sharks

Coral reefs are like the busy towns of the oceans with many amazing creatures living in and around them, including sharks.

**Whitetip reef sharks** spend their days resting under coral ledges and in caves. They come out at night to hunt small fish, crabs, and octopi.

Other reef sharks are **blacktips** and **grey reef sharks**.

**Caribbean reef sharks** rest during the day and hunt at night.

The **draughtsboard catshark** has a handy trick to fight off **predators**. It hides in a hole in a rock and sucks in lots of water to make itself swell up. It is very hard for a hunter to drag it out of the hole!

Many different sea creatures rely on coral reefs, so it is very important that these beautiful parts of our oceans are looked after and protected from harm.

The **coral catshark** lurks in holes and caves.

23

# Glow-in-the-dark sharks

Sharks are such amazing creatures that some of them can survive in the deepest depths of the ocean where it is really dark and gloomy.

**Lanternsharks** have glowing spots on their bodies.

**Blackbelly lanternsharks** have glow-in-the-dark tummies. They swim in large groups, or **schools**, very deep in the ocean.

We need to see each other so we can stick together.

The **velvet belly lanternshark** has two spines that light up. These look just like lightsabers!

Deep-sea sharks have very large eyes. They need them to take in as much light as possible in the dark water. This helps them spot each other, catch food, and avoid being dinner for **predators**.

**Kitefin sharks** are the biggest glow-in-the-dark sharks. They can grow to be as long as a human man is tall.

The scary-looking **cookiecutter shark** uses its glowing tummy to get the attention of bigger fish or seals. Then it takes a big round bite out of them!

**Bioluminescence** is the word that describes the light made by living organisms.

# Gentle giants

Here are some huge sharks! They are not at all dangerous to humans, even though they are GIGANTIC.

The **whale shark** is the BIGGEST shark in the world. It can weigh as much as three cars!

It is so gentle that divers can swim alongside it!

The **whale shark's** favorite food is tiny sea creatures called **krill**. It swims along with its mouth open and gulps in lots of water.

The water goes back out through its gills, and the **krill** get trapped there. It is like using a giant sieve, or filter, to collect food.

**Krill** are about as long as a pinky finger.

Scientists think that **whale sharks** sometimes snooze on the seabed for a few weeks at a time. This saves their energy until they want another **krill** dinner.

Zzzzz ...

The **basking shark** is the second biggest of all the fish in the world. It also filters its food through its gills.

**Basking sharks** have huge, dark **dorsal fins**.

They are called **basking sharks** because they feed near the surface of the water during warmer months, and it looks like they are sunbathing!

**Megamouth sharks** are very mysterious. We really do not know very much about them, because we hardly ever see them.

They seem to spend their days very deep down in the ocean and then come up to the surface to feed at night.

Most sharks have jaws under their head, but **megamouths** have jaws at the front of their body.

Hey! How would you like it if I called YOU megamouth?

# Sharks in the past

Sharks are very, very ancient creatures. They have been on our planet for HUNDREDS of MILLIONS of years. They were here even before the dinosaurs were stomping around.

**Fossils** are the stony remains of animals and plants that died a very long time ago. They are like clues showing us what they were like and what they did.

BUT sharks do not leave behind **fossils** in the same way as other animals, because their skeletons are made of **cartilage** and not bone.

Most of the clues about ancient sharks come from their fossilized teeth.

**Great white shark** tooth
(Actual size!)

**Megalodon** tooth
(Actual size!)

**Megalodon** was one of the largest **predators** ever to have lived on planet Earth. It was about 66 feet (20 m) long! This is more than three times the size of a **great white shark**.

Human

My name means "massive tooth!" Watch out!

Megalodon

Great white shark

It had two kinds of teeth.

**Hybodus** was a prehistoric shark that lived in shallow seas.

Sharp ones for ripping into **prey** ...

... and flat ones for grinding up the shells of shellfish.

**Stethacanthus** seems to have had a very odd fin that looked just like an ironing board!

29

# Mystery sharks

Deep in the icy oceans of the North live some huge and mysterious sharks. Like the other giant sharks living today, they are not dangerous to humans.

**Greenland sharks** live in the coldest oceans on Earth.

No one knows very much about their habits except that they swim VERY, VERY slowly. They spend most of their time VERY, VERY deep down in the freezing cold water.

They also eat all kinds of stuff, including things that are already dead. They are **scavengers**.

They like nothing better than the rotting, smelly old carcass of a dead whale or seal. Yuck!

Every now and then one gets caught in a net, and scientists try to find out more about these strange creatures.

Scientists use a special technique which can tell the age of a shark from its eyes. They think that **Greenland sharks** can live to be hundreds of years old!

They could be some of the oldest creatures on Earth, and are not fully grown until they are 150 years old. This is when they can start to have babies.

Happy 200th birthday, Mom!

# Do sharks have friends?

Most sharks live and hunt on their own, although some do like to gather in large groups. There are also some much smaller fish that like to spend time with sharks!

**Hammerhead sharks** sometimes gather in huge groups called **schools**. This is so that they can meet a mate and have baby sharks.

Some sharks go on long journeys called **migrations** to find a mate or a safe place to give birth.

**Blue sharks** swim thousands of miles every year!

The **cleaner wrasse** is a very useful friend for a shark. This little fish swims right inside a shark's mouth. Then it cleans up bits of old skin and pesky things like sea leeches.

**Remoras** are also called **sharksuckers**. These fish have suckers on their heads. They attach themselves to the tummies of sharks for a ride or to catch scraps of food.

I'm sticking with you!

**Pilot fish** swim close to sharks so that other **predators** will not get them. They also eat up leftovers from shark meals.

**Orcas** are definitely NOT friends with sharks. They sometimes hunt and kill them.

# Sharks in danger

Sharks are in great danger from humans. Not many people are killed by sharks, but humans kill MILLIONS of sharks EVERY YEAR.

Sharks are killed to be eaten ...

... in dishes like shark's fin soup.

Shark liver oil is used to make cosmetics.

A shark's are hunted for sport.

They are often caught with other fish in fishing nets and then just thrown back into the sea.

Old, dumped fishing nets are also deadly traps for sharks.

Sharks are the top hunters, or **predators**, in the oceans. They do a very important job keeping the balance of life in all the seas and oceans of our planet.

SAVE OUR SHARKS!

There is still so much we do not know about sharks and how they live. The more we can find out, the better we can protect them.

Scientists use special gadgets to track sharks. This helps them study how far and where the sharks are going.

To help, raise awareness by finding out more about your favorite sharks and what is being done to keep these fascinating and amazing creatures safe for the future.

# Special shark words

**Ampullae of Lorenzini** are tiny pits on the snout of a shark with sensors that detect the electrical signals sent out by other creatures.

**Barbels** are special whiskers that pick up the tiny vibrations made by creatures under the seabed.

**Bioluminescence** is light made by living organisms.

**Camouflage** is how an animal blends into its surroundings so that it cannot be seen.

**Cartilage** is the bendy, gristly stuff that sharks have instead of bones.

**Dorsal fin** is the fin on a shark's back.

**Denticles** are the pointed scales that make up a shark's skin.

**Embryo** is the name for a growing baby creature that has not yet been born.

**Fossils** are the stony remains of animals and plants that died a very long time ago.

**Krill** are tiny sea creatures that look a bit like shrimp.

**Migrations** are long journeys made by creatures, like sharks, to find new feeding grounds, a mate, or a safe place to give birth.

**Oxygen** is the gas that humans and other creatures need to breathe to stay alive.

**Pectoral fin** is the fin under the front of a shark's body. There is one on each side.

**Predator** is a creature that hunts for its food. Sharks are top predators!

**Prey** are the creatures that predators like to hunt and eat.

**Scavenger** describes a creature that eats things that are already dead.

**School** is the word used for a large group of sharks, or other fish.